Midnight Divination
and Other Wayward Hobbies

poems by
Angie Kimmell

Acknowledgments

The following poems have been previously published, performed
&/or displayed
(with much thanks):

Art & Words Collaborative Show--*"After Clearing the Speck of Mojave from My Third Eye," "The Night Leonard Cohen Followed Me Home from Cannon Beach"*
Denton Writes: Versifico--*"From the Back Porch in Beaverton, Oregon," "Re-membering"*
Galaxy of Verse--*"Walking Meditation"*
Merging Visions Collaborative Show--*"Walking Meditation," "Hands On," "Summer Day Mosaic," "Takeoff," "Family Tree," "Wanting"*
National Federation of State Poetry Societies--*"Family Tree"*
North Central Texas College--*"February Commute"*
Poetry Society of Texas--*"Domestic Anticipation," "The Night Leonard Cohen Followed Me Home from Cannon Beach"*
Poetry Society of Texas: A Texas Garden of Verse--*"In the Summer of No You," "Walking Meditation," "Mrs. Adams"*

Dedications

For Birdie & Sandy.
I could not have
accomplished this Big
Dream without you.

And for Tuco,
who never takes "no" or
"I can't" for an answer.

Thank you.

About the Author

Angie Kimmell has lived in Washington, DC, southern Germany, Oregon & Texas. She received her BA in art from the University of North Texas, but is now a Jill-of-all-trades; when she's not writing, she's reading, photographing, painting, building, hiking, playing music or sometimes actually working her day job.

She is a lover of metaphysics & philosophy, dream interpretation, human nature, pondering our place in the universe & all things odd & quirky.

She firmly believes the meaning of life is to experience true happiness, spread lovingkindness & communicate with others.

Ms. Kimmell is active in many visual art & poetry collaborative groups, displays in gallery shows & performs her poetry regularly at events. Her work has been awarded & published at state & national levels.

Angie lives in a little house on the lake in Denton, Texas, with her four-legged children & her soulmate, Tuco.

Contact her at:
happylittlesparrow@gmail.com

Contents

Midnight Divination

I've made such melodramas—farce
& folly led my life.

Midnight Divination

Crosslegged on a couch of night,
I see the hand I hold is marred
by slashing line of jagged white.
I hope that I am in that scar.

Perhaps it's Fate, or in the stars--
like moths to amber lamps of light.
We cannot change our draw of cards
crosslegged on a couch of night.

Through Mound of Venus, passion's plight,
your love line was extended far
beyond intended length. Tonight
I see the hand I hold is marred.

I've made such melodramas--farce
and folly led my life. This bright
wound cheers. My listless soul is jarred
by slashing line of jagged white.

A gently tracing nail, a quiet
afterthought, a second chance. Our
entangled fingers, eyes invite
the hope that I am in that scar.

My flustered breath and jaded heart
are ribcaged sparrows craving flight.
Your white-tailed love line speaks: we are
to hold this moment in delight,
crosslegged on a couch.

A Man Without Freckles is a Night Without Stars

Skin spread beneath my palms.
A tanned coastal hide or
the pulpy page of a child's puzzle book,
all jumbled dots and tattooed lines.

You taste of the sea, love.
The Gulf shadows are flickering,
tiny silver fish quiverdancing along your back.

I am tracing constellations slowly,
slowly, dot to dot in dizzy lamplight,
the scent of salty dusk and musk trailing
my teasing, tickling nails.

I am drunk on our creation.
The kings and queens,
hunters, boars.
The snakes and cranes are
licked and twined to life along your body.

We are fantastical creatures of perfect match.

Tiptoe

Shhh...Tuco is sleeping.
He lies lightly in peace.

But I want to climb into
his gentle exhalations
as a tiny ball of light &
be breathed to the stars,
to curl between his large hands
& rest like a comma
in childlike prayer.

I want to dance along his arms,
pinpointed & permanent,
with the tattooed snake shadows
of second chances.

But now is the quiet time
of tiptoed floorboards,
of unfurled brow,
of rabbit eyes jumping
under lids of dream.
Now is the time
to nestle in the blanket
of Mother Night.

Shhh...

5

First Words

"I wish we had met when I was seven
and you were two,"
you breathe in warm morning puppybreath against my neck

         & I wake to images of
       you & your brother riding bikes in a
        street of sun & me in diapers.

      "We would have nothing in common,"
        I say & roll to face you.
      "What if I were seven & you twelve?"

You scrunch your furry face.
 "That would just be weird.
What if I were twenty & you were fifteen?"
you ask & gently touch my hair with your large hand.

       I watch the bamboo shadowdance
      through the window across your face &
     think of the trouble we would have caused,
       the paths we had chosen,
        parallel but separate,
    only to cross perpendicular at this moment--
     experienced, clearminded & ready.

      "I think we met at the perfect time,"
         & I smile.

Galveston in November

dyed candypink hair
a perfect match to that strange
Gulf Coast bloom you plucked

First Christmas

My soul's a tangled string of lights
unraveling from my laughing smile.
Admiring our first tree tonight,
my soul's a tangled string of lights.
I'm dizzy, love, so hold me tight
& share this tangent moment while
my soul's a tangled string of lights
unraveling from my laughing smile.

Gulf Coast Eyes

The miles I go toward your arms,
catlike anticipation bunching in
muscular white heat,
strip of burning summer asphalt
stretching down my spine.

The stopping, starting,
painful stopping;
the combusted scent of
liquified dinosaur bones.

I'm infatuated with this journey,
the progressive trail of smells:
northern prairie Denton to
sticky blackhot Dallas tar to
pungent pine Jasper to
oily plastic Houston to salty
ocean fish Galveston Bay.

Oh! The miles I go toward your shiny lure,
your honey brown pierwood,
golden sunset on wet sand eyes!

Water Witch

We never should have drank the water
she gave us. Bottled in green & glinting
like a mischievous eye, tied with a
perky bow, sparkling, fresh, healthy.

I had my misgivings, eyed it as a
naughty dog sitting innocently on the shelf.
Then the cold, rolling cycle of New Year's Eve.
Our perfect celebration sealed with
a toast from this cursed & slender bottle.

Cursed? you say. Cursed! See
how this young, lithe witch has
poured between us, poisoning you
with sparkling attention & me
with the dregs of paranoia. See
how her cursive namecard has embedded
distrust on my heart & Salomed around yours.

The traditions read that New Year's Eve
signifies your future in the coming year.
How can the spell be undone?
Our previous perfection replace this distaste?
We never should have drank the water
she gave us.

Attachment

I have been protective of our love,
& I love you too much. I have gripped so tightly
its breath has strangled in its gentle throat.

Perhaps it is the winter, with her
cold bleak days filled with
murderous crows perched & choking
the arterial networks of
tree branches scratching a last grasp at
the gray landscape.

Or that we are the rising & setting
of day & night. The sun & moon have
relations, true, but they never
taste the others touch, merely
waltz & pass in antiquated courtship.

And maybe I have been inactive, stagnant
as swampwater. My mind occasionally,
momentarily cleared by a random fresh stream,
screams a muffled underwater
Stop! through muddy clumps & bubbles
of confusion. But I am easily swallowed
by soft comforts of guilty silt &
quicksand lethargy. It gives me time to
worry over obsessions; like currents they
polish smooth my stones of paranoia.

I struggle, a raw mudwoman, but remain sticky &
slowly consumed on the foul, remorseful
shoreline. Stop. I need your understanding pull.

From the Back Porch in Portland, Oregon

So much has occurred in so little time.
I squat here, barefoot in the chilly evening
alone completely
for the first time in my life.

I've lost all that was worth something:
my soulmate, partner, best friend.
I count the days by cigarettes.

Dizzy, empty, spent
a year will tick by,
measured by rain, crisp, cold hikes

365 packs
4300 cigarettes

I miss your eyes, your shoulders
your laugh.
I can't smile anymore.
I sleep on the couch
and dream of you walking through the door.

Half-

-awake. Slowly rolling
to your cold ghost-memory form.
Bedside table standing
sentinel over our photo.

-pot of coffee. Hopefully counting
the filters until you come home.
Kitchen counter patiently planning
arrangements for your milk & sugar.

-empty closet. Expectantly waiting
for your clothes to fill its echo.
Lonely hanger stoically holding
the black hoodie I took that still smells of you.

Nightsweats

My heart offends me, I shall pluck it out
with clutching hand, a digging bloodbone,
a finger tracing aortic meat route.
My heart offends me, I shall pluck it out.
Night rough as cat's tongue, secret spout
of lifeblood, darling darkling. So alone.
My heart offends me, I shall pluck it out
with clutching hand, a digging bloodbone.

Distance

I have purposefully decided to pine.

Rather than let go
I embody Browning.
I lose myself in the worship of you.
There is no other, Beautiful.

Rather than enjoy community
I prefer Dickinson
& watch as a small wren from my window.
I am an island without you.

Rather than live, love and medicate
I embrace Plath,
contemplating the Great Unknown
that lies beyond the oven racks.

I am fear and loneliness
I am remorse and loneliness
I am holding out--barely--
but only for you.

I've Lost You

I know I've lost you.

My sunshine is gone;
I took it for granted,
all the while complaining of the heat.
I've already forgotten your laugh.

A Silhouette of Mourning Doves

against a
Maxfield Parrish sunrise.
Brighter than tinfoil,
pinker than bubbles
--surprise--
a Klimt Kiss dream.

Eyes open wide.

Blind shadow slats,
sheet folded flat,
dark angles where
angels once lay.

I thought of you today.

I've mastered the fine
art of mo(u)rning.

In The Summer of No You

I pace my small floor
as a harried inmate,
my fingers bit to bone.
Carpet trail of matted flatness, ashes,
Pollock-like drips of coffee stains
punctuated by black dots of cigarette burns.

I sleep by the pool
seemingly carefree,
my skin dark as a laborer's.
Eyes closed to expansive blueness, cloudbanks,
I will the sun to bleach and fade
my tattooed body to single, gray-green color.

An important Japanese scroll left to the elements.

I roll over our memories
as an elephant in its graveyard;
bones of recollection shined smooth with revisiting.

I page through mental snapshots
as an ancient widow.
They are pliable, idealized,
frayed at the edges.
Antique scrapbook faces
kissed and caressed for what seems like a century,
touched and loved into unrecognizable oblivion.

To the Escape Artist

I distrust trust. Once well
constructed, now crumbling,
crumbling to disgusted dust.

I've rebuilt guilt. All the
lessons learned forgotten,
our bridges lie burned & sodden
from the deluge. I'm now careful,
carefully squelching our
past to filtered silt.

Wishes

This is how I did it,
how I survived.

Picture a square white ream
like a brick or heavy heart.
My hands flew in a secret sign language,
repetitive days, folding 1000 cranes.
A cut, blood. A wish & tears.
A crease, peak & bend.
Listen for the silence that was a cat but for
the incessant dead skin swishing of paper.
See? I strung them end to end,
dry rustling woodpulped Spanish Moss
throughout my home, a wafting white
curtain of loss caressing ritual pacings.

Lie back with me in night black as oil.
I counted stars & stars between stars,
my skin indifferent to cold, my cursed
breath fogging, each star a
shining tooth in your smile.

Feel the mocking Spring appear overnight.
Bradford Pears sprouted white old man tufts
of bloom. The dandelions, in their evolution,
jeered with their brightly nodding, silly yellows.
We know! We know! they sneered as I
patiently waited, then destroyed.
Puffs of flowerheads, soft as my kitten heart &
wasted breaths of wishes. The daisies fared
no better. Nervous, bloodbitten fingers
tore the tender buds to nicotine stained shreds
in the wanting of your lithe, calloused hands.

But I had forgotten the darkness that lurks
behind the false pretenses of your soul.
I quickly bundled your laugh away
into a tiny packet of pocketed memory.

Those cloaked in midnight robes who click
beads in stone hallways would whisper that
God did for me what I could not. But I see now
 it was my wishes; they were for something
else entirely. The slash of you went deep in this
springtime suffering, sure, but quickly faded to a
paperwhite scar, a space between stars,
the nothingness of seeds & petals in the breeze.

Fooled by the Interloper

I should have been suspicious
from the beginning; you had
no tattoos.
No self-inflicted pain of permanent pleasure.
No happy wrapping of doodled paper
or scribbled journal of your soul
or pectoral medals proudly penned.

I stripped you, regardless,
in the twilight middle ground of my lamplit room.
You, my pristinely over-bleached hair shirt,
a perfectly pink newborn rat,
a pale, tree bark larvae dug from dirty leaves
& licked clean.

& I still let my legs say yes,
even as you traced the white scars
of my inner thighs
& questioned the scrolls of my arms
& read the roadmap of my back.
I was limp in the heat of your flat summer eyes.

But I have learned to be cautious,
in the end, of wounds
that are hidden mystery,
that lurk in the mealy rotten core of the mouth
& lie in wait, their pathetic haunches bunched.
They were scrimshawed all along your spine
& etched indelibly from scalp to toenail
in invisible ink, layered & coded,
lemon juice white on paper white skin.

He Knew 100 Ways to Kill a Heart

"I'm not trying to hurt you," he said,
& she pictured her sweet, sensual, fragile grape of heart

squeezed to pulp in his fist of hand
burst under nonchalant heel like a full tick
withered to a raisin in the sun of sarcasm
masticated & spat between sneer of teeth
dissected & pinned to the black wax tray of scalpel wit
peeled bare as a serial killer victim
dropped & rotting on the floor of apathy
scraped into the refuse of unwantedness

"I'd hate to see what would happen if you *did* try," she said,
& closed the door gently behind her.

The Exact Moment My Heart Broke

I run the purple sunset with
1000 knives at my back.
Betrayal sharp as chrome
flashing, a flashing watereyed sun
bright as panic.
My heart is running, but
not running. My soul is waiting, but
not waiting. My mind not knowing,
but learning to hold my heart
more secret than dream.

Keys of Regret

Hand clinging to old metal
tied by string.
Star-shot eyes blinking, blinking
shutter-fast across
black primordial creek.

Keys of momentum
swinging, swinging
string tracing
invisible smiles
through cold burning air.
Faster, faster,
then release--

the five-fingered
letting go of you.

A distant whimpering,
soul-crushing splash.

Back turning, wind pushing,
brown rusty eyes blinking--
stabbed by shards of tear.

The Science of the Soul

You say, "I will always love you, but
it will take time before I can trust you again."

You say this as if we have some kind of a future together.

I say this:
For years my soul has been crushed
by a cold, hungry black hole
of a fist. For a decade I routinely told my soul,
Be strong. Maybe someday this grip will loosen.
On good days, I could feel her shift
ever so slightly in her bonds,
a small and dormant beastie with
her own tiny heartbeat.
On bad days, she was
absorbed in void. There was only the
clenched anger of your hand.

Let me tell you:
I've pried your fingers open and I've rescued
her. I've been cradling her gently in
my own hands after tenderly massaging her
fragile body back to life with bravery.

And let me tell you also about your precious space,
both the real and the metaphoric:
I am no longer downcast. My eyes look up
and out now. They see rabbits in the moon, romance,
old men, passionate lunacy. Not
your lifeless rock scientifically orbiting the Earth.

And this:
the stars are queens, dragons, dot to dot lions, perhaps
even the glowing ends of the gods' cigars. They are not
your gaseous balls of cold light.

My vacuum-sealed creativity is a supernova of
maniacal, non-analytical behavior. My mind expands
and bursts its boundaries. My spirit is
once more a questioning rambler.

They are an active part of this world again.
They are at peace.

Domestic Anticipation

A heart can be mended. Under the covers of gentle, lamb's wool
Nights, I thought I heard the repetitive click of needles,
The frayed, unraveled muscle fibers knitting together again.
In the bright scream of morning sun, I've been consciously
Cleaning my spirit in rolled sleeves, bound hair, tied apron.
Imagine a once-loved home in broken, dusty disrepair,
Polished sparkling new with tears. But here it is:
A powerful, rustling flutter of swallows in
The freshly swept chimney of my soul again.
I'm eagerly bending down the ticking days
On nimble, able, thimbled fingers again.
Now, my dears, you are welcome.

Comparative Religion

My cathedral arches with the sunrise,
my Sunday Best a muddy pair of comfortable shoes.

Comparative Religion

I cannot take comfort as most.

Those who carry leather-bound myths
through echoing hallways,
silent & fearful in their Sunday Best,
regarding human-written fiction as fact,
wearing smooth their strings of beads
with guilty, nervous fingers.

My cathedral arches with the sunrise,
my Sunday Best a muddy pair of comfortable shoes.
The damp, earthy lakeshore serves as my pew
while I hum my song with the choir
of birds & frogs & cleansing breeze.
My congregation is a motley group of sassy squirrels,
lines of ants & rustling mangroves.

No one is ever quiet &
everything is soul-shaking.

This is my holy place.
Here I find comfort.

The Night Leonard Cohen Followed Me Home from Cannon Beach
an automatic writing in response to "Hallelujah"

I heard the song for the third time this week.
In the doctor's office waiting to prove my sanity:
In the rustle of plastic trees swaying in air conditioned corners:
In the angelic hum & glow of fluorescent lights: *Hallelujah*!

& I am transported to the dark, winding tree tunnel of US 26.
The claustrophobic pines arch over their secrets.
The omnipresent pines flex their black knotty fingers in the wind.
Those hateful pines scratch out the eye of the jaundiced moon:
Hallelujah!

So we sit at the edge of the country--facing West, facing Nothing.
We sit as the greedy tide sucks our toes under cold February sand.
Below oppressively rolling, malignant night clouds,
we sit in ominous roaring void, connected & small: *Hallelujah*!

Our trek across the wasteland beach ends in misadventure.
Haystack Rock is an unattainable hunchbacked mirage.
It is the oracle of the ocean, waiting to be questioned.
It is a bent knee on the spread legs of Mother Earth: *Hallelujah*!

The growling Pacific pushes us back to crushing clutch of pines.
In infinite midnight silence, Leonard crackles through the radio.
In damp, heavy silence, wet, black forest rushes by foggy window.
In comfortable silence, your hand seeks mine in the dashboard
glow: *Hallelujah*!

I heard that song for the third time this week.
My flatlander heart felt peace one solitary, dark magic night.
My stained glass heart is a shining beacon against wide Texas sky.
My lifeline heart throws a rope across the country & pulls:
Hallelujah!

Birdie

Your Sister Spring and Mother Cardinal
offer hope in this life's carnival.
Her sunrise beak, her calls are integral
to Sister Spring, your Mother Cardinal.
And when your love and joy are nominal,
coincidences cast to marginal,
breathe in Spring and Mother Cardinal
to give you hope in this life's carnival.

Greenbelt Solace

A gentle swath of sunny fields
lies dry & hot with underscent
of gathering storm & thunderclouds.
Unraveling horse trails beckon me
to bless my boots with miles & time,
explore the path before the rain.

But tell me, what's a little rain
when Mother Nature gives me fields
to wander, calls to me in time
of sorrow? Acrid underscent
of cleansing ozone comforts me
beneath the Payne's Gray thunderclouds.

The berries twine toward thunderclouds,
they're ripening purple in the rain.
This blackened bit of life in me
takes solace in these vines & fields,
in subtle growth & underscent
of tartness turning sweet in time.

I find a grove unseen by time,
oasis greened by thunderclouds,
with knee-high grass & underscent
of wildflowers specked with rain.
The slender trees grow toward the fields,
a bowing bower guiding me.

There's still small light that shines in me,
regardless of this darkened time.
I roam the pristine prairie fields
in solitude with thunderclouds
to bring my heart into the rain
of bitter brushy underscent.

My flower bouquet has underscent
of ancient hide, reminding me
of family bibles in the rain.
I'll press these buds one at a time
in memory of the thunderclouds,
of lost religions & the fields.

The underscent is real this time
& blankets me with thunderclouds.
I lie in rain & breathe the fields.

Summer Day Mosaic
(in yellow monochrome)

Pumpkin Seed Peanut
in Cantaloupe Sunrise,
Banana Cream Sun Porch
with Lemonade Straw.
The Glistening Gold
of Bumble Bee hair--
cute as a Duck's Bill!
Soft Butter tires
on Yellow Brick Road,
a Sun Burst Canary Song,
an Afternoon Glow.

Run After the Storm

damp concrete & dimness
rainsmell & mooncloud
oak trees dripping lucid darkness

streetlights humming angel mantras
cicadas revving chitin engines

crickets singing here here here here

electric curtain of sound pulsing pulsing
feet running running
breath carving up the butterthick night.

Walking Meditation

I hike with steady purpose
heel toe heel toe
the strata of time below my feet.
If I am careful, I can feel
continental plates shifting
like grinding teeth in the night.

I breathe in measured lungfuls
in two three out two three
the trees inhale as I exhale.
If I am quiet, I can hear
atmospheric ties pulsing
like sleeping lovers sharing air.

I gaze on hazy distance
hills or clouds? hills or clouds?
the mountains stand guard and shelter me.
If I am patient, I can see
sentinels of rocks eroding
like ancient mothers giving all.

heel toe
in out
hills clouds

Everything is shifting.
Everything is connected.
Nothing is permanent.

All Saint's Day

Fallen limbs
jumble of bones.

Long, low logs lie
as fallen soldiers.

Blackened trees
sentinels over
crumbling powder of
dead leaves

their rusty, dusty children
now earth--
color of blood.

Stratacycle

applecrisp November sky aquamarine watercolor wash flat, yet
infinite curtained backdrop for a

milehigh cloud bank Jet-Puft accumulation of breathing ponderous
entity shifting earthward toward the

mimicking treeline greenorangeredgold fingerpaint explosion
whispering leafsecrets held by

windrubbed branches creaking like sneaking on floorboards at
midnight merging, conspiring to

unified trunks, dark infantry ranks guarding jewelgreen mystery
root-toes dipping into a

slowcreeping river thick as sleep trailing tree roots like hair
holding, immersing me on my

back, a floating Ophelia, pale lotus hands--open bright peaceful
eyes--open reflecting above on the

applecrisp November sky aquamarine watercolor wash flat, yet
infinite.

Winter Field Mosaic
(in white monochrome)

She lies glittering, silent. A Pearl Star or
Pearl Necklace, an Ivory Lyric of Bones.
A Silver Silence--Distant.
A Paperwhite rustling flight
above Mosaic Canvas,
new with Origami Angels
crowned with Ashen Halos.
March across the Winter Frost,
lovely Chalky birds of December.
Show me life in this Eternal Freeze.
Forge your Quiet footprints like
trekking Knights across my Winter field.

Winter Fog on Lewisville Lake

And the lake sleeps,
a furry deathbed daguerreotype
or the blank void of spirit
passing between two lives.

She sleeps
with her aged skull hidden
beneath downy white pillow
and arthritic toes curled
under thick bleached quilt.

The lake sleeps,
only black Live Oak stumps
of fingers exposed to cold pristine damp,
gnarly knobs clutching
the bedcover's edge.

And I think
all winter I have foraged, starving
for color, visually feasting
on red toxic berries
and dead orange leaves,
all the while missing
the sustenance of the stark absolute.

Endarkenment

I want to fall in love again with life.

Endarkenment

I cannot walk today. The woods are dark
& full of boars. The Live Oak trees have turned
to knitting needles on the outside of
the starving window. Screech & click, they perl
the fog, explode the Rorschach grackles from
their meager perches to the right & left.

I cannot walk today. The barren path
will drag me to the lake--so hungry in
her loneliness--with clacking seashell teeth
& frothy lips that gnaw along the shore.
But I am always underwater, cold,
slow-moving & surreal. Uncomfortable,
a stranger in this box as mute as fish.

A palish sun rolls nervous eyeball at
the grinning, skullwhite solstice of the moon.
I huddle leeside of the deadbolt. Cold
is constant in my heart, but these are times
of little deaths, endarkenment & sleep.

And if my February heart survives,
I'll pick the healing scabs, preserve them in
a labeled Mason jar & break the seal
wide open come the lean November winds,
this memory scattered in the autumn leaves.

Moonsick

The moon, she casts her sickly shadow
in my heart--my love pales sallow.
On fevered forehead, plowed yet fallow,
the moon, she casts her sickly shadow.
Sister sun shines a jaundiced yellow
and sends my soul a flight of swallow
but moon, she casts her sickly shadow
in my heart--my love pales sallow.

Portland Pines

I am here and you are here
but you're not really here
in this lonely, claustrophobic little town
the only way I see is down
six feet under in this wet and muddy ground.

I breathe my name in morning air
to hear it and remember that I'm there
but then it vanishes--a ghostly, foggy memory of mine,
elusive dream and small design--
drifting upward toward the canopy of pines.

I'm back home but I'm not home
with you not here it's not quite home.
Arranging things and waiting for your call,
I stop to pause within the hall
and feel our souls connect across the silent lull.

Now I see it's not the place
but what's inside I've come to hate
and all the things I loved I'm growing to resent.
I thought life would be different
on Columbia and muddy Willamette.

Today's the Day Things Fell Apart

The stitching's come undone
along the edge of hemmed felt heart.
The damage has begun.

Zipper mouth is jammed wide open;
teeth refuse to mesh.
Sticky, rusty words are spoken
in musty dimestore breath.

Button eyes, once beetle black,
dangle from a thread;
goggle-gaze at foot of sack-
cloth--pensive, dusty, dead.

Cotton skin is stained and brittle--
the stitching's come undone.
Seams are stretched now, holding little.
The damage has begun.

Life Tectonics

Saw me in half,
you'll find 38 rings--
many starved and thin
from catastrophic droughts
of unhappiness.

But what is my tiny, human sadness
to the trees?
They breathe in as I breathe out--
that is all.

Dig in my chest,
you'll find a small shell--
once fragile, now ossified
from strata upon strata
of disappointment.

But what are my aspirations
to the ceaseless rivers?
They chuckle cynically
over rocks and trailing limbs--
hiding stone secrets
under their beds.

Climb into my mind,
you'll find continental plates
of shifting thoughts,
incessant peaks and valleys of delusion.

But what is my anguish
to the stoic mountains?
They stand sentinel,
majestic in their wizened indifference.

I am but a mote, a microcosm in time,
a single cell in the Grand Scheme.

Melancholia Dramatica

Bleak sorrow has constructed a
concrete cell around my tender heart.
Oppressive in my chest,
a ventricle vault,
it will always be with me.

Despair has bound a
bulky ball & chain to my birdlike leg.
Restricting all flight,
a clamping shackle,
wherever I go, it drags behind.

Its painful presence looms above my
unmoving, horizontal body.
An ominous weight,
a dismal sack of sodden sand,
whoever I'm with, it crushes the both of us.

My plates of food are cooked in woe;
the ponderous peas languish beside
the melancholy pats of butter
melting miserably over the potatoes.

& when I smile,
Black Plague gloom oozes from
among my teeth.

I hear its menacing underscore
in every song.
I read its secret message between the lines
of every book.

Desolation will be with me forever.
I am it & it is me.

Wanting

I want to fall in love again with you
& long & lingering licks of kisses; plant
my heart beneath the willow trees at dusk.
With open mouth, I want to gently taste
the incense of your neck again & sway
in revelation--or was it summer breeze?--
& later, bare-entwined & tickling, have
you pull me closer in your sleep, exhale
& dream together of our growing old.

I want to fall in love again with art,
possess two painted rainbow hands of one
who births & breathes the beauty into life.
To lose myself in linseed oil dream
& lick my brush in thought & taste the earth.

I want to fall in love again with god
& walk the jewel-like lakeshore dark in new
moon night. To celebrate the singing stars
& find my joy again in startled flocks
exploding in calligraphic flight.
To keep this tiny speck of stardust me.

I want to fall in love again with life.

After Clearing the Speck of Mojave from My Third Eye

I count endless infinity in threes--
a mantra, quiet incantation. Spell
bound, pyramids of men & minds & cells
within the crosscut timbered pinion trees
grind to a halt in awe of galaxies
created over silent desert hills.
I count endless infinity by threes--
a mantra, quiet incantation, spell.

My sitting lotus form organically
mimics a perfect triangle; foretells
the power of the body, thought & well
of spirit. Under starlit canopy,
I count endless infinity by threes.

Hands On

8000 miles away
from fluorescent classrooms
shuffling texts
page-sized squares of black & white images
she meets her subject, this ancient wall
in full color
in awesome, towering glory.
Student of amazing, tragic life.

Eyes closed against dizzying sun,
palm pressed to hot, rough stone,
she absorbs radiant heat, memories
from thousands of others
from thousands of years
who have done the same.
She can feel their fingerprints
rising to meet hers.

Cryptic writing pulses
with energy under her touch;
a heartbeat left by another seeker,
a mark on a tree to keep her on the trail,
to find the way Home.

She is not learning.
She is remembering.

Her human instinct like elephant to graveyard.
Ancestry flowing from hand to heart.

Reflections Upon Waking the Last Day of Thanksgiving

This recent nesting phase--
the painted porch,
the updated Amazon wish list,
the extra thrift store blankets
& kitchen table centerpiece--

the many small comforts lost to many poor choices

do not point toward attachment,
but healing.

Polarity

Polarity

Instead of bacon,
I'll order the Fak'un
because
sentient beings are
numberless
and
Instead of Camera 1,
there's always Camera 2
that shows you
the real side
of you
and
Instead of enlightenment,
I like endarkenment
which trips you,
oblivious,
into your grave
and
Instead of The War,
there's always The Game,
which is basically
a posturing of
the former
and
Instead of a star,
I see constellations
that whimsically spin
dot-to-dot
world view
and
Instead of G-O-D,
there is D-O-G
who holds
all meaning
in his pink secret smile.

Homeward Bound

Portland rain has got me crazy,
gutter punks are downright lazy.
West Coast mindset,
got to forget,
Granolier Than Thou is what we call it.
Windshield wipers beat the time
to Johnny Cash "I Walk the Line."
Gorge & sky the shade of tin,
summer heart in winter skin,
wind my way to Pendleton--
Oh, I'm Texas bound!

Oregon highlands,
stench of meth labs,
gave up all the things that I had.
White line blindness,
I'm My Highness,
free again & you're the minus.
Cross the border, head to Boise,
winter wind is cold & noisy--
Oh, I'm Texas bound!

Salt Lake City's
just so pretty
in the sunrise, it's a pity.
Singleminded,
smell of brine &
got to leave all this behind me.
Truckstop ramblers,
scratch-off gamblers,
Laramie is full of amblers.
Convoy with my semi friends,
hang a right--I'm south again--
Oh, I'm Texas bound!

Nebraska, Kansas, Oklahoma:
all these square states are so windblown.
Speed suggestions,
farming lessons,
tractor pulls & God's great blessings.
Reservations,
Cherokee Nation,
tuned in to my Dallas station.
Cross the Red & taste the wind,
kiss the ground, I'm home again!
Oh, I'm Texas bound!
& I ain't never gonna leave.

Takeoff

I close my eyes, the vessel slips--
weightless, skybound, birthed by growling melody;
100,000 humming, monkish lips
pressed against the ripeness of a mother's belly.

Weightless, skybound, birthed by growling melody,
flying back through time toward yesterday.
Pressed against the ripeness of a mother's belly,
a heavy weight of predawn gray.

Flying back through time toward yesterday,
there's roaring waves inside the engines.
A heavy weight of predawn gray
is pushed by winds, the ocean grins.

There's roaring waves inside the engines--
100,000 humming, monkish lips.
I'm pushed by winds, the ocean grins,
I close my eyes, the vessel slips.

February Commute

The cars are wearing jaunty snow toupees.
Rolling huddled silhouettes in icy white,
they creep toward work through heated windshield haze--
a line of cheery headlamps piercing predawn night.

Rolling huddled silhouettes in icy white,
they confidently glide through swirling snow--
a line of cheery headlamps piercing predawn night.
Orion points the way for them below.

They confidently glide through swirling snow
with tires shushing, breath exhaling from behind.
Orion points the way for them below,
these small, mechanical souls personified.

With tires shushing, breath exhaling from behind,
they creep toward work through heated windshield haze.
These small, mechanical souls personified--
the cars are wearing jaunty snow toupees.

Rollover

You lie on your side,
wheels still spinning at
the silver sky,
on a curved bridge
of predawn gray,
underbelly exposed
like a beached whale
or a petulant dog.
Powerful machine
kicked
into tin can coffin.
Commuters
impatient with inconvenience
on their lives,
unthinking of yours
swinging
from the dull gold pendulum
of the rising sun.

"The Pleasure was All Ours, Mr. Bradbury--Thank You"
*found on a chalkboard sign in front of a used bookstore upon the
death of author Ray Bradbury*

"Ray? When did we meet? And where?"

A gangly, girly Sixth Year Summer. My grandparents maze of
North Carolinian home. A stern-faced dresser squatting in sun-
strewn, dust-moted room. Gaping, open mouthed drawers filled
with paperback teeth. I devoured you. I closed my eyes, tasted
dandelion wine, smelled the jungles of Venus, felt the rattle of a
mental rocket launch, felt three months of warmed floorboards
beneath me.

Do not despair, beautiful sir; the daily lives of monster families
will continue to turn on the spines of dusty paperback wheels in
October country. Illustrated men will immortally haunt travelers
with inked stories of rockets and space, of madness and sideshows,
of technology and death of the soul. Mischievous twelve year old
boys filled with the insight of fifty year old men will run through
endless Illinois fields. Montag will perpetually rest on his bed,
ponder his eternal matchbox (GUARANTEED: ONE MILLION
LIGHTS IN THIS IGNITER), light a match, blow it out, light a
match, blow it out. A writer, cloaked in his bathrobe, cloaked in his
prime, will wander down the stairs, enter his library and cry,

"My God, did I write that? Did I write that? Because it's still a
surprise."

And he will sit at his desk and continue his story.

Re-membering

I function fine.

Through dream you shine,
my phantom limb.

An itch begins.

A roar of love--
the darkness of
a phantom sea.

Reality
will come with sun--
what's done is done.

For now we lie,
you by my side,
attached and whole,
a shoulder-soul.

Englyns of the Dreaming Deep

I'm dreaming of your teeth. In sea of black
the scallops float beneath
a gingival seaweed wreath.
Your tongue hides in its sheath.

Your long toe speaks of love in the liquid sand.
A plump and rosy grub
it curls, signals darkly of
mighty mysteries above.

A nail shines in starlight--mother of pearl.
Shadow puppets play-fight--
clam shell hands spread against night,
catch the moon and take a bite.

Eulogy for a Nameless Black Cat

I anticipated you each morning, like clockwork,
your presence disturbingly large,
pantherlike in your solid midnight coat,
eyes the setting of Mars at dawn.

You crossed at our corner, looked both ways,
cunning, bright,
slick as oil slinking the silver-dewed horse pasture.

I reveled in your dark magic acrobatics in those fields,
your slyly wicked, ridiculous hunting pirouettes & pounces.

I saw you this morning at our corner,
but flat, undignified, your face a scream of death,
your satin side marred by cartoon tread marks.

Know that I will honor you daily
in my kindness to your brethren
& mourn your sleek black energy
& still anticipate you each morning, like clockwork.

Om Mani Pet Me Hung

breadloaf kitty
zen with tucked paws squint-eyed,
furry Buddha

Bee Bush

summer-skinned knees
climb linoleum stairs
8 year old hands
with kitchen trash duty
(but momma, i'm playing!)

humid press of August afternoon
sun a sharp holler high in the sky
(everyone feels dead)

ebb & flow tide of
alarm bell cicadas
crinkle of shedding skin
tinfoil in the ears of morbid stillness
clinical white sun rolls observant eye
radiant hot pavement spiderweb of stone
(if i miss all the cracks, they won't get me)

closer, closer
slipping silent
clasp of small hands on plastic
or are they claws
closer, closer
fever hot terror
closer, closer
moving fast
a last red brick turn
(it's just a stupid bush)

looming largegreenancient
furred gut-watering black
striped panic yellow
closer, closer
moving weight
hungry swarm
gathering insect hum
(oh, momma i can't i can't i can't)

one sharp scream
then droning buzz

East Texas Cookin'

I am the envy of the girls in Lost Pines.

My Momma tells me to "Take heed, my child,
and listen well, because your looks," she sighs,
"Will never lead a man to your home or side."

A greasy book of recipes is mine.
It's passed along our matriarchal line.

So now, with just a single verse I wind,
just a word can call a man, a single rhyme
will grab him by his stomach and spellbind
him to my kitchen, my honeycombed surprise,
my dark and yeasty, needy love divine.

Those girls can never match my voodoo kind.

Family Tree

I've got my Momma's legs.

These sturdy Live Oak trunks are made
for lifting children, chasing dogs
and loving husbands.

I've got my Momma's legs.

My feet are firmly planted flat
against the Mother Earth. Ten toes
curl deep like knotty roots--to anchor
me through storms, to weather drought
and hungry times.

I've got my Momma's legs.

Like Tolkien's Ents, I stride through life
with proud and ponderous gait.
Protector of the Innocents,
I wield my strength with care.

And if we stood in sunny meadow, hip to hip,
with arms branched high toward sun
and fingers brushed by wind,
we'd be a mighty grove of four.

I've got my Momma's legs.

Mrs. Adams

My daughters, I was created specially.
The birds, beasts and even man
sat up from filthy spit and dust.
I was carved of gleaming bone
taken from that secret dark
beside my husband's heart.
Ah, how I loved that man!
Even as he neglected me for friends,
even as he took my love but never gave,
even as he whittled my specialness away
down to bloody, bone-root marrow.
Forgive me, my sisters, for causing you pain!
I only intended a rift between them,
to keep him home and by my side.
Instead, I lived with the heavy image of
pointing fingers, pointing fingers,
my helpmate standing idly by,
kicking at the dust like a petulant child,
voicing his betrayal to save his dirty skin.
Instead, I lived to churn out
famous sons and nameless daughters
and die a lonely, infamous scapegoat
in a story written by men for men.

Beautifully Wild

to the next generation of female poets

women or girls
my daughters
sisters fair
(oracles of the 21st century)

biting teeth &
words of pearls
my mentors
whipping hair
(4 Venuses on stage)

you speak
critiques
of subtlety of
sneaking sexism
(don't stop)

when boots step
on your necks
(don't stop)

when hands of man
shut your mouths
(don't stop)

when life & lovers &
lack of faith
leech like shadows
on your time

Don't. Ever. Stop.

21st Century Howl
Dear Misters Ginsberg & Solomon; It's getting worse.

Urban coyote startled in the dark side street, slouching under the
glow of garish stadium light;
slinking car to car across vast expanse of parking lot, shocked into
awesome incomprehension
by the Wal-Mart that wasn't here yesterday;
by the razed, trash-ridden lots;
by the plastic bags skitting in the wind like lost souls;
by the deliciously evil smell of fast food.
The road to Hell is paved with Chik-Fil-A;
the road to Hell is walked by hollow spirits with heads bent over
iphones, they fall into pits,
the Fool card of Tarot, their heads marked with 00, a terminal
pandemic case of cranial rectitis.
Is there a pill for that?

In mass-produced sweatshop sweatpants,
in Hummers, they drive 2 miles to yoga-fusion classes;
in search of spirituality & peace of mind;
in search of a way to burn off the GMO factory-raised Super-sized
Taco Deal, the guilt of exploitation.

Addicted to medicine companies tell them they need;
addicted to medicine no one can afford;
popping pills in the infinite sameness of cardboard MacMansions;
in subdivisions named after the Nature killed in order to build
them;
ticky-tacky homes of Thousand Oaks built by immigrants who
think they want the American Dream;
where the children take Ritalin;
where the husbands take Viagra;
where the wives take Valium;
where the heavenly blue glow and angel hum of TV permeates all;
where the crinkle of paper bags and squeak of Styrofoam replaces
the dinner bell.

80

They lay down to sleep in Indonesian-made sheets--tossing &
turning all night through their dreams:
the 14 Mexicans who built their home but sleep in one room;
the animals crammed so tightly in cages you couldn't swipe a
credit card between them;
the small children hands sewing yoga pants for 10 cents an hour;
the cancers & AIDS waiting for cures while society clamors for
more hair, less weight;
the cliched Starving Children who have never heard rustling paper
bags or squeaking Styrofoam cups.

American Family rolls over in their sleep and primal instinct
infiltrates subconscious thought:
the freedom of cooking their own dinners;
the freedom of not being a slave to technology;
the freedom of walking, of breathing untouched green forest air;
the freedom of independent thought, of self-sufficiency;
the freedom of not believing everything you hear.
"Think Outside The Box" is not just a marketing campaign.

In the dark, midnight meanwhile, urban coyote scavenges the
parking lot for wasted french fries
& howls & howls & howls at the loss of his Thousand Oaks.

Big Box

small urban coyote
this sudden rash of Wal-Marts
has startled me too

crash

for many years
I have made
pretty words
with you,
naively, perhaps,
unwittingly
placing faith
in plastic objects,
never doubting
silver
rivers of wire
winding
deeper courses
ultimately eroding
into
grinding
halt.
i am struck
by this grasping
at
intangible illusion,
this clinging
to
electric impulse &
virtual
nonexistent
words,
this moaning woe
that
all
is
lost.
there's
plenty more
where those
came
from.

Fin*

While I lie down,
feigning sleep,
I have a desperate urge
to call you
to invite you
to my home
to tell you why I
feel like I do.
To tell you that
if you were a cat
I'd cut off your whiskers.

*Fin** was my very first attempt at writing a poem. I was 16 at the time & the token "weird art kid" at my high school. I had just had my heart crushed by my first unrequited love, Jeffrey. To this day, I still think there is no worse feeling in the world than unreturned affection, although many years have passed & I am no longer upset at poor Jeffrey who was, no doubt, probably scared by my intensity.

I was a prolific visual artist, with grand plans to attend art school upon graduation. This night, however, I could not paint. Or draw. Or do anything but listen to The Cure cassette I owned over & over. Thus began my long-term hobby of writing in times of artistic angst.

Sitting on my antique bed in my room that was the entire second floor of my parents' historic 1896 Lampasas home, I entertained all the cutting witticisms I could say, plotted all the petty, teenaged ways of revenge. Needless to say, I followed through with none of them & Jeffrey & I remained friends until graduation.

This was the night, though, listening to the shushing of traffic two stories below, crying & writing my little heart out, that I found an alternate release, a way of verbal—rather than visual—expression.

It's funny to me that the roles have reversed with time. Decades later in my adulthood, I wear the many hats of artist, maker, photographer & musician, but I turn to poetry first.

I hope you find some joy in my work, some comfort & inspiration. Perhaps you can relate to much of what I have to say. If so, I hope you feel not as alone with your feelings, that I have given a voice to the parts of your soul that you may be afraid to say aloud.

Love & light to each of you. Namaste.

Angie Kimmell
March 2014

32667212R00058

Made in the USA
Lexington, KY
28 May 2014